Ordered Steps

A Poetic Walk through my Thoughts and Life Experiences

Vernell Diamond II

Table of Contents

Ch. 1: Love...6

Ch. 2: My Faith..17

Ch. 3: My Thoughts and Life Experiences.....................37

Ch. 4: Tributes...61

Ch. 5: Short Story Poems..................................67

Acknowledgements

To my loving parents, Vernell Sr. and Angela, thank you for being my guides and inspiration.

To my Pastor, Pastor Craig, thank you for being one of the greatest mentors in my life.

To Laretha, Theresa, and LaTasha, my sisters, thank you for looking after me as your own.

To my brother Kevin, thank you for being a great role model.

Introduction

Imagine if there was a list of poems that could show others a piece of who you are. Well, that is what you will find throughout this book about myself. Although this is a book of poetry, it will seem more like a book of many stories. Firstly, these poems are based on several subjects that fall into various categories, but they will reflect off of my thoughts and life experiences. Readers will view a plethora of poems about faith, love, tributes, triumphs, trials, and much more.

Secondly, my goal in this book is that all can relate to it, and that it will help them to get through their problems. I hope that others can learn from the things that I think about, or that I have endured.

Lastly, this book wouldn't be in existence if it weren't for my Lord Jesus Christ. Since he is my life, he is surely in my thoughts and has been a part of my life experiences. So for that, all the glory goes to him. I hope that all readers will enjoy reading this book just as much as I enjoyed writing it.

Ordered Steps

One

Love

Poems about love, marriage, and relationships

What is Love?

Written by: Vernell Diamond II

What is Love? Is it a force unseen? An emotion, an action, or a simple thing?

What is love? Is it a person or place? An overwhelming feeling, or a filling of space?

What is love? Is it a state of mind? Is it a sudden memory, an advisory, or a sign?

Love, what is it? A sacrifice? A word of wisdom, or giving someone a chance at life?

To know what love is, discover its Creator, know its purpose, and find the activator.

A tree grows tall and strong through its course, but behind the growth, water and sunlight is the source. So does love grow as a tree of life, with its branches of grace stretching far and wide. Its leaves bringing shade to comfort us and the roots strongly grow in surplus.

Who is the Creator of love? Jesus, the Christ, the Son of God, the Father of life.

He is the author of love. He paid the price. His sacrifice gave us eternal life.

So, what is the purpose of love? To bring all people together. Love unifies our hearts to the will of the Father. We are one family that must care for one another. This love is pleasing to the eyes of the master.

What is the activator of love? It is simply action. Love is not just words with little satisfaction.

Lastly, what is love? Where does it begin? To discover it, you must look deep within.

Where is it in the Bible? I Corinthians 13

She's on my Mind

Written by: Vernell Diamond II

Is it my fault that marriage is on my mind; a covenant so sweet, just, and divine?

Is it my fault that I'm in love with my wife; her charm, and her countenance which is in my delight?

How can I love a woman whom I don't know? How can imaginary thoughts comfort my soul?

I need someone who is unknown, for I endlessly resent being alone.

I'm too young, you say, but time is too short to wait. I have to search and find a worthy candidate.

My mind is made up. I'll find my love. I'll search for her with guidance from above.

I'll love her with a love unfailing, a love unconditional, and a love prevailing.

Her identity is hidden, but she seems so near. I declare our relationship will surely be sincere.

So is it my fault that I love my love and cherish marriage; a covenant pure as a dove?

I don't know who my love is. I don't know the woman that I will find. However, one thing is clear, she's on my mind.

Where is it in the Bible? Proverbs 18:22

Love, United

Written by: Vernell Diamond II

When two fervent hearts mend, affectionate love begins.

The two becomes one in a settled blend.

However, if the hearts contain dissonance, their love will fail.

Only unity will cause their love to prevail.

Love united is love everlasting,

It's as strong as hurricane winds blasting.

Love that is spoiled becomes bitter tolerance, and separate hearts rends a house divided.

Fight for love and embrace it with care, for the absence of it is destined despair.

Do not blunder, carefully ponder this great wonder.

For if God has joined your heart in love to another, let no one put your love asunder.

Where is it in the Bible? Matthew 19:5-6

My Heart Aches for Love

Written by: Vernell Diamond II

My heart aches for love.

My heart yearns for marriage.

My mind questions its arrival.

My soul longs for a bride.

My mouth sings of her coming.

My thoughts wonder of who she is.

My desire is to marry my better half.

My duty is to provide for my soul mate.

My intention is to love her with all of my heart.

My goal is for our relationship to prosper with God as our guide,

But I must wait until that day comes.

Lord, give me patience!

Comfort my aching heart that aches for love!

When the day comes, bless me with a bride.

Fill this missing rib in my side.

Reward me with my good thing.

Although my heart aches for love, I will remain patient until she calls for me.

Where is it in the Bible? Genesis 2:18

When She Comes

Written by: Vernell Diamond II

Why does my soul cry out for a bride?

Why do my emotions flow for her, which I cannot hide?

Why does my mind think of her as if I've known her before?

I don't know her, but the thought of her, I can't ignore.

Awaiting her arrival is very rewarding,

But also painful and truly abhorring.

Anticipation for her knocks at my door,

But the wait is long for her, whom I long to adore.

The time will come when I will meet my bride,

and my hunger for love will be satisfied.

The just matrimony will be set in place,

With God's hand covering us always.

Nonetheless, that time is not now,

And I must have patience on the journey somehow.

There's a rib missing from my side waiting to be filled,

And when she comes, my prayer will be fulfilled.

Where is it in the Bible? Genesis 2:24

Simple Love

Written by: Vernell Diamond II

Love isn't complicated. It's very simple.

When activated, love causes all to tremble.

As for relationships, don't be dismayed.

Companionship, surely God has ordained.

Marriage, don't forget it, so your love will be righteous.

God smiles on a relationship that is just.

Conversation is the key. It brings reconciliation,

For relationship without communication is bound for separation.

Care for your mate. Serve them in humble submission.

You're no longer two but one so work as a unit.

Don't be bitter. Have faith to find your love and let Christ be the center.

Seek direction from above.

Trust in God, he'll guide you to your friend.

As that time comes, may your love endure to the end.

Where is it in the Bible? Colossians 3:18-19

Virtuous Woman

Written by: Vernell Diamond II

I want a virtuous woman, who lives in truth,

I want a virtuous woman who is modest in her youth.

Her ways should be righteous, joyous and bright,

In Christ, she puts her trust and finds delight.

I need a virtuous woman, who connects with me,

On several matters we should agree.

We are two souls that will become one,

And we will serve God's gracious Son.

I want a virtuous woman who discerns and observes,

And God our Father; she will serve.

I want a virtuous woman, but I pray,

That I will be the virtuous man fitted for her one day.

Where is it in the Bible? Proverbs 31:10-31

Don't Awaken Love Early

Written by: Vernell Diamond II

My brother, don't awaken love early.

My sister, don't ignite the flame of love before the time.

Young lovers, love is delicate and mild.

If it is rushed without wisdom, it can falter and become desolate.

Bachelors, let God guide you to your wife.

Widows, remember that God is the restorer of love and holy matrimony.

Nevertheless, among all, intimate love must not be rushed.

It is as a sweet fruit at harvest time, but the fruit must be removed only when ripe.

A fruit removed early is bitter, so will love be if rushed.

Love is patient, and kind.

So don't awaken love before the time.

Wedding Night

Written by: Vernell Diamond II

How fair and lovely is a wedding night?

A night filled with passion and sweet delight.

A night cherishing the one that you love,

A night establishing a holy covenant made above.

On this night, the stars will shine brighter than the sun,

For two separate hearts will become one.

Their bond will be made and tightly sealed,

And the introduction of their love will be revealed.

How mild and tender is a wedding night?

A night lasting without fear or fright.

A night that is hard to ever forget,

When two lovely souls are able to connect.

Man and wife will be matched together,

And their song will hover in the skies forever.

Their hearts will pulsate as a single beat,

And the consummation of their marriage will be complete.

How beautiful and precious is a wedding night?

A night that begins a future, very bright.

A wedding night starts a marriage off right,

For the bride and groom, side by side, may now unite.

Where is it in the Bible? Hebrews 13:4

Marriage Defined

Written by: Vernell Diamond II

Marriage is one of the most honorable commitments in the sight of God. It was the first covenant ordained by God. God takes marriage seriously, but our modern world takes it lightly. The world doesn't honor marriage because they don't understand its values. Please understand what marriage is. The definition of marriage is the legally or formally recognized union of a man and a woman. It is also the combination or mixture of two elements. A man and a woman from totally different backgrounds and walks of life become one being. Two stories become one.

Marriage is as two rivers joining together at its peak forming a great ocean. That ocean is filled with life and death. It is filled with calming waves and wild storms. It has the brightest days and the darkest nights. However, God is always in control over the current. Marriage is filled with love, commitment, sacrifices, laughs, tears, prayer, and patience. The modern world seems to avoid having so much responsibility with one mate. Furthermore, they claim that God's rules inside of a marriage are too strict, so they strive to re-establish those laws. That is the work of the enemy.

If God planned for a man and a woman to join and become one through marriage, of course Satan would strive harder to break what God has mended. So if you think that your marriage is in shambles, don't worry. God can fix any problem. Adam and Eve were kicked out of paradise, and they didn't get a divorce. They stayed together. Even after losing two sons, they had another named Seth, which would bring about the lineage of Christ.

Never give up on your marriage. Try to work through your problems. The secret is to agree with each other. How can two walk together unless they agree? Sunlight must agree with water to nourish soil. The soil must agree with the seed to form a plant. The plant then becomes a tree, but the tree must agree with water and sunlight to grow leaves. Any two things must agree to work together, but if they don't, they won't prosper. Therefore, man and woman must agree on various matters for the matter to be resolved.

Marriage is as two strings in a tapestry and the third string that holds the first two together is God. The third string binds the first two becoming one broad cord that is not easily broken. The other cords in this pattern are the lives that are affected by the marriage creating a quilt, a beautiful tapestry telling a magnificent story. So my questions for the happily wedded couples are, what is your story, and whose lives are you affecting? Lastly, do not let what God has brought together to be put asunder.

Where is it in the Bible? Ephesians 5:22-33

Two

My Faith

Poems about Jesus Christ and the Bible

Woe to the Flesh

Written by: Vernell Diamond II

Woe to the flesh and all of its desires!

Woe to its lust which leads to hellfire!

Woe to the flesh and its chains of sin that arrest
holy hands of love and discipline.

Woe to the blasphemous mouth of the flesh,
breathing lust, debauchery, malice, and incest.

Woe to the spirit of fleshly things, which opposes
the righteousness of Christ our king!

Woe to the flesh, the promoter of sin, the destroyer
of morality, and the heart of abomination.

Woe to the devil, our defeated foe, and to he and his
fallen angels I strongly declare woe.

Glory is to God and shame to Satan, for God lives
forever and Satan's end is destined.

Blessed is he that yearns for Christ, and his holy gift
of eternal life.

Understand and know, for those that yearn after the flesh, its wages lead to eternal woe.

Woe to the flesh.

Where is it in the Bible? Galatians 5:19-21

You're My Everything

Written by: Vernell Diamond II

A simple prayer to our Lord.

Oh Lord, Be my vision,

Be the head of my life,

Help me in my every decision.

Be my strength,

Be my faith,

Be my joy,

And be my grace.

Be my provider,

Be my friend,

Be the one on whom I depend.

Be my God,

Be my guide,

Be my shadow under which I hide.

Be my encouragement,

Be my shield,

Be my blessing in the city and field.

Be my example,

Be my savior,

Be my Lord,

Please, shadow me with favor.

Lord, you are my everything, and most of all you were my sacrifice,

So I will serve you, Lord Jesus, for the rest of my life.

Trust in the Lord

Written by: Vernell Diamond II

Don't depend on mortal things in your life.

Don't you know that the things of Earth are temporary? Money, fame, and other material things will fade. Yet, what will happen when you close your eyes for the last time? Your possessions will fade. What about your soul? Things you see are temporary, but things you don't see are eternal.

Don't tend to the desires of the flesh. Understand that the nature of every human seems right, but can be extremely evil. The flesh is as grass to be cut down and thrown into fire. It is as weak as a man without food or water. It is as evil as the fallen angel himself. It hungers after every form of lusts and when that lust is fulfilled, it hungers for more. It can never receive enough. It will never be satisfied.

Don't trust in humans and human nature for guidance in life. Trust in the Lord with all of your heart. Keep your trust in the one that created the dimensions of the universe with his words. Trust in the one that sits on Heaven's throne and uses our planet as his foot stool. Trust in the one that blew the breath of life into his creation. Trust in him that aims to save you instead of human nature that wants you to endure temporary pleasure, for its ways lead to destruction.

I would rather trust in an infinite, almighty, and omniscient God, than to please a body of dirt with earthly desires and possessions that last only for a season.

I beg of you to trust in the Lord.

Where is it in the Bible? Proverbs 3:5-6

The Resurrection

Written by: Vernell Diamond II

The body was wrapped.

The tomb was sealed.

His disciples surely mourned him.

He died, and the hope of mankind was buried with him.

All changed when the angel of the Lord appeared preparing his entrance.

The enormous stone rolled away easily like a tumbleweed rolls through a crop field.

There, the Ancient of Days stood with all power.

His feet gracefully stepping on solid ground,

His eyes glancing at the Earth's landscape once again,

His countenance was as brilliant as the rays of the sun,

His clothing was greater than the fine linen of Egypt.

His might and power withstood death.

His blood forgave our sins.

His resurrection sanctified us.

When he rose, hope rose again with him.

He is Jesus Christ.

He is the way, the truth, the life, and the resurrection.

Where is it in the Bible? John 20

The Rapture

Written by: Vernell Diamond II

The Earth quakes and the people shake, at the brightness of his coming.

Hearts' pound as the trumpet sounds, announcing His arrival.

People stare and are scared, and many start running.

For they lament that this event, is the beginning of their survival.

The angel's voice is loud while on a cloud, Jesus makes his appearance.

God's son has finally come, for his church, beautiful and bright.

For the many that aren't ready and don't have holy countenance.

This is the day that they will pay, for not walking upright.

Billions fly into the sky and are caught up in the air.

Sons and daughters, mothers and fathers, are forever to be with the Lord.

No more crying and dying for the saints, and no more burdens to bear.

Happy and delighted, the saints are united, with their God on one accord.

In an instant, they vanish as the Earthlings panic, on where they went.

Broadcasters scuffle and their feet shuffle, to find answers and stories.

Families are missing, and people are wishing that they would have listened to messages the Bible sent.

They don't understand that in the land, this is the beginning of their worries.

While Earth travails, Heaven prevails, as the saints enter the city.

Jesus walks and others talk, as they all march in.

No sorry for tomorrow, and no more pity.

There is no dismay, for today, life in paradise begins.

Where is it in the Bible? I Thessalonians 4:16-17

The Essence of God's Love

Written by: Vernell Diamond II

Your love is magnificent. It is as precious as a newborn, but it's as strong as a mighty warrior. My heart is whole because you have mended it. My tears are gone because you, my Lord, have wiped them away. Your love has forgiven all of my filthy sins, and your grace has forgotten them.

Jesus, I thank you for your love. You have sent it so gracefully to me even though I do not deserve it. Your matchless love and immeasurable grace has rested upon me like a blanket. This is why I cannot contain my praise, because your love, King Jesus, has consumed me.

This is my prayer Lord. Help me to share the same love that you have placed upon me.

Where is it in the Bible? John 3:16

The Comforter

Written by: Vernell Diamond II

The Holy Ghost is the comforter that was sent from Heaven to Earth,

To ensure that men will live forever, starting with a second birth.

It came swiftly to holy people chosen by the savior,

A presence powerful enough to cleanse all sinful behavior.

The comforter is not human but a spirit indeed,

A spirit that is holy and has the power to redeem.

This comforter simply yearns to sustain and correct,

And every man who accepts it, his life will it direct.

This comforter is Jesus; he is the Holy One,

Father, Spirit and the only begotten Son.

He is the comforter full of grace and truth,

And he comes as a gift wanting to live inside of you.

The evidence of his spirit is speaking in tongues,

A harmonious melody that is sweetly sung.

This heavenly language connects us to him.

Therefore, our prayers will rid us of a life that is grim.

Always remember that the comforter is our Lord,

He connects our spirit with his on one accord.

And if you allow the comforter to guide your heart,

He will lead your life into a righteous new start.

Where is it in the Bible? John 14:26

Repent, God Forgives Sin

Written by: Vernell Diamond II

Anyone one who has ever lived has committed a sin. The only one without sin is Jesus himself. All have sinned and has come short of the glory of God. However, God gave us a practice that will reconnect us to a holy lifestyle. He gave us repentance. Once we surrender to God's will and allow him to save us, we have an advocate with the Father. This means that if we fall and ask for forgiveness, he will forgive us. If we fall to the ground drenched in sin, we shouldn't stay there lying in defeat. We can stand back up and repent for our sins and try again.

Condemnation and guiltiness are not a good feeling. It is not healthy naturally or spiritually. The devil wants us to feel like God will never forgive us for our sins. However, if he can forgive a former mass murderer like the Apostle Paul, he can forgive anyone. Have a heart of repentance. If you have done wrong, don't allow your mind to soak in a bath of misery.

Repent and don't return to the sin. Yes, we will feel guilty if we backslide. We feel terrible enough to think that God won't forgive us, but he will. He forgave David for his eloping with Bathsheba. He forgave Joseph's brothers for selling Joseph into slavery. He forgave the children of Israel for going after false gods. Above all, he forgave the sins of the whole world when he died at Calvary.

So why weep and pout? "Lord, forgive me for I have sinned," is worth more to God than a thousand tears. Repent and turning from the sin is better than feeling condemned. Don't fret if you have fallen. God will forgive you if you ask. He loves you and cares enough to forgive you for any sin that you commit. Furthermore, he will give you Holy Ghost power so that you won't return to the sin. Therefore, do not ponder over the problem my friend, for repentance is the beginning of the solution.

Where is it in the Bible? Acts 2:38

Lucifer the Ignorant

Written by: Vernell Diamond II

He was once Lucifer, the anointed cherub of God. He was a mighty archangel in Heaven. His countenance was bright, and he was covered in various precious stones. His being was made of pipes where music proceeded. He was perfect since the day he was created, but because of his beauty and rank in heaven, he became proud. Lucifer began to exalt himself before God himself. He wanted to sit upon the mount of God claiming to be greater than God. Foolishness became the countenance of Lucifer. His pompous attitude became his downfall. How can the creation be greater than the creator? A guppy isn't greater than a shark. A cat isn't greater than a lion. Therefore, an angel will never be greater than the master of the universe.

Lucifer seemed to misunderstand that. So in wroth, God withdrew the brilliance found in Lucifer and all of his authority and rank in Heaven. He became as desolate as a dry desert. His pipes no longer praised God with glorious music. They will forever spew a sad and dreadful tune. His countenance is as low as the dust on the earth. His head is a resting place for the heel of the Son of God. God evicted Lucifer from the Kingdom of Heaven along with all of his followers. One-third of angels fell from Heaven that day along with Lucifer. His flight was as lightning.

This is why God hates pride, because pride caused this anointed cherub to become a fallen angel. Now Hell is Lucifer's eternal resting place. His place of dwelling is where the worm doesn't die, and the fire doesn't cease. The lake of fire is his bed, and the smoke is his bitter fragrance. His pipes are filled with a tune of evil, and his countenance breathes iniquity. He was Lucifer, the anointed cherub. He became Lucifer, the ignorant. Now because of Christ, he is Satan the defeated.

Learn from the story of Lucifer. We have a chance of receiving eternal life, but if we condone ourselves as Lucifer, we could end up where he will spend eternity.

Where is it in the Bible? Ezekiel 28:13-19 and Isaiah 14:12-20

How Great is God's Love?

Written by: Vernell Diamond II

How great is God's love?

It reaches higher than the peak of Mount Everest,

And it lunges deeper than the lowest ocean depths of the Atlantic.

How great is God's love?

It stretches farther than the Great Wall of China,

And it is wider than the nimbus clouds that float in the heavens.

How great is the love of God?

It is stronger than an elephant's ivory, but it's as delicate as a newborn child.

God's extravagant love surpasses all things.

It breaks yokes and mends broken hearts.

It sets captives free by breaking the horrid chains of bondage.

How great is God's love?

It was great enough to save me.

Honor the Master

Written by: Vernell Diamond II

Please don't disrespect my savior,

Don't blaspheme against the name of the Creator.

To you, he's just a god or some deity,

But in my eyes, he's my everything.

For every event of distress and disaster,

The blame is always put on the master.

Humans never take the responsibility,

For their transgressions and filthy debauchery.

However, they blame the Lord, and some even deny his existence.

They break God's laws without a guilty conscience.

Other gods seem to gain more respect than he.

Jesus usually receives Earth's scrutiny.

I hate that these things are true.

Yet, it has been this way for a long time and is nothing new.

Nonetheless, don't dishonor my God. He has done no wrong.

If you don't want to honor his name, then leave him alone.

Leave the name of Jesus as a name to be praised.

Let his name be honored always.

God Called the Youth Too

Written by: Vernell Diamond II

God is God, and he chooses servants,

These servants perform his will,

That all people would come to Christ,

And the scriptures would be fulfilled.

He uses old wise men,

He uses women of truth,

He uses prophets to speak his word,

But he also uses the youth.

God calls the youth by name,

To use them for his purpose,

He anoints them and teaches them,

Until their gifts begin to surface.

Some believe that the youth are simple,

Or not ready for God's use,

"They are too young to say anything,"

Is usually their excuse.

Does God set a limit of age?

Did he only use the old?

If that was true,

Half of the Bible wouldn't be told.

David was young when he fought Goliath,

Jeremiah was a child,

Samuel heard God's voice as a lad,

Very meek and mild.

So why is there much lack of faith,

When it's God using the young?

Even Jesus was thirty when his ministry begun.

God called the young,

Because they are strong,

They are working in his purpose,

Where they belong.

Don't doubt the youth,

Don't doubt their potential,

Don't act like you are with them,

But your true feelings are confidential.

Trust the young men,

Encourage them with gladness,

Listen to the youthful women,

Celebrate their deeds in happiness.

When God uses a young one,

Don't turn your head,

If you look away too long,

You might miss a word from God instead.

Elder saints in Christ,

Accept the young congregation,

You are their inspiration,

And they are the next generation.

You were young once,

You were given a chance,

And now you're established in Christ,

In whom you strongly stand.

So don't crush the youth's faith,

They are trying to live for Christ,

Just like you,

They yearn to receive eternal life.

For the seasoned in Christ,

I thank God that he called you,

But always remember,

God called the youth too.

The Man that Killed Death

Written by: Vernell Diamond II

Who is the greatest foe known to man? The answer is Death. Many have fallen into the hands of Death since the beginning of time. Many kings, priest, prophets, prime ministers, and much more have lost the fight to Death. When sin came into the world in the Garden of Eden, Death was loosed from its chains throughout the world. Death was a large dog in a shallow space of time, barking at the doors of existence. When Adam and Eve ate the forbidden fruit, the chains were released, and Death busted through the doors.

There was only one man who could put a muzzle on Death. He is Jesus Christ. A dog should never approach a lion in battle. That is why that dog called Death made a mistake approaching the Lion of the Tribe of Judah. People make the mistake thinking that the cross was an execution for Christ. That moment was really an execution for death. Death died at the cross and was buried as Jesus rose. The greatest foe lost its life that day, and Jesus took the keys to its burial chamber. For in the end time, at the judgment, Death, Hell, and Satan will be buried in the lake of fire for all of eternity. They will have a grave that they do not own.

Death is no longer the greatest foe, but the weakest. With the Sword of the Spirit, and by the blood of the Lamb, Death was cut down. That dog was put to sleep, and the Lion reigns in victory. Jesus is the man that killed death and the God that gave the world a chance at eternal life.

Marriage Supper of the Lamb

Written by: Vernell Diamond II

My eyes await for the day that I am able to see that fine wedding table. I want to sit across the table where the saints will feast with the Lamb of God. After we have gone through the gates of Heaven and settle, we will feast and celebrate the holy marriage between the Church and the Lamb.

We will dine, talk, feast, and celebrate the reconciliation between the saints and their God. My seat is surely reserved for the Marriage Supper of the Lamb. Is your seat reserved?

Where is it in the Bible? Revelation 19:7-9

All for Me

Written by: Vernell Diamond II

Sometimes I wonder why you would die for me. Although I know the answer because your word explains it plainly, I still wonder. Why? Why did you do it? I can imagine you praying in the Garden of Gethsemane. There you knelt praying and pleading with the father to let this cup pass. Nonetheless, you encouraged yourself and gained enough strength to speak the words, "Not my will, but thine will be done." You knelt there worrying while your sweat like drops of blood trickled down your face. The drops hit the ground as heavy raindrops in the spring. Alone you prayed while your disciples were asleep and there wasn't a human around to comfort you so an angel had to be sent. Why did you put yourself through all of that trouble?

I can imagine you in the court room of the Sanhedrin. There you proclaiming yourself as the Son of God, which is true, yet you were mocked for it. They hit you, and they spit on you like you were a dog. They pulled your beard out of its place, and they wrongfully accused you of being a blasphemer. Why did you go through with it? Why, Lord Jesus, would you accept their actions and give yourself into their hands?

I can imagine you at Pilate's court being tried for treason. You were standing as the defendant, the Jews as your plaintiff, and Pilate as your judge even though you are the Almighty judge. You were accused wrongfully. There you stood Lord Jesus, and your people pleaded for you to be crucified. You are the creator, and your own creation wanted you dead. However, you stood there steadfast and unmovable awaiting your horrid fate. Why? Pilate didn't want you to be crucified. So his form of mercy was to have you flayed. You were whipped until your skin was no longer attached to your body. You were sheared as a sheep going to be slaughtered, and after all of that, the Jews stilled wanted you crucified. Why did you let them do it? You could have easily asked for a legion of angels to come from Heaven to protect you. Your words alone had more than enough power to cause your enemies to kneel at your feet, but you decided to remain silent.

So they placed a crown of thorns on your head, mocked you, gave you your cross, and made you carry it to your own execution. That's like a lamb putting a knife in its mouth and bringing it to the same man who's going to kill him. As a matter of fact, that's exactly what happened. The Lamb of God willingly offered himself up to be a humble sacrifice for people that rejected him and for a world that didn't know him. However, you still persevered. Why?

I can imagine you walking down Golgotha road, and I wonder what was going through your mind knowing what was about to happen. I can see you on that hill called Calvary, where they nailed your hands and your feet. I can see where they nailed the title you deserve above your head, "Jesus of Nazareth, King of the Jews." I can hear how you screamed in agony when they stood the cross up and your body began to hang, and your bones popped out of its joints. Nevertheless, you still went through with. Your heart-broken mother is watching as you die slowly. Your disciples are hopeless. You stayed on that cross until you gave up the ghost. Why did you do it Lord? That was my question, until I read John 3:16.

"For God so loved the world that he gave his only begotten son, that whosoever believeth in him should not perish, but have everlasting life." That is my answer.

God, you loved me so much, that you gave your only son to die in my place. You gave your lamb so that my eternal home wouldn't be a burning hell. You did it so that one day when I die or when you come to Earth for your church; you can look me in the eye and say, "Well done, my good and faithful servant." That is why you died. That is why you went into Satan's domain and took his keys. In three days, you rose from that rocky grave. You rose with all power of Heaven and Earth in your hands, the same hands that were nailed to the cross. You did it all for the world to have a chance to live eternally. You did it so that we can be reconciled to the Father. Thank you Lord because I know the answer now. You did it all for me.

Three

My Thoughts and Life Experiences

Weary Road

Written by: Vernell Diamond II

A sinful life is a weary road, filled with strife and fear.

Its lanes are drenched, with an awful stench, of anguish so severe.

A sinful life is a weary road with highways of despair.

Its way is wide, for all to ride, as long as they can bear.

A sinful life is a weary road that seems so sweet at first.

As time flies, the sweetness dies, leaving bitter thirst.

A sinful life is a weary road that denies morality.

Its wages of sin has a horrible end, a grim eternity.

Life is a road and sin makes it weary, but a holy life brings peace.

A life of Christ brings a future-bright, with all of your burdens released.

War within Myself

Written by: Vernell Diamond II

There is a war occurring within myself between the flesh and the spirit.

The spirit wants to please God, but the flesh wants to please itself.

The spirit yearns for righteousness, but the flesh seeks sin.

The spirit abides in holiness, but the flesh saturates itself in filthy lust.

How majestic is the spirit that breathes the anointing of Christ and eternal life?

How selfish is the flesh, rather pleasing itself instead of God?

These two war within me daily.

These two fight fiercely within the depths of my soul.

The spirit tends to help me and ensure my salvation. The flesh wants to lead me to eternal damnation.

Yes, the two fight in a continuous war, but I declare from this day forward, that the war has ended.

The spirit is victorious.

The Death of Anger

Written by: Vernell Diamond II

It is as a poison that runs through my veins. It is a burning heat that rises through the depths of my soul. It is as fierce as a roaring lion, and it cuts like the teeth of a shark. It is my sworn enemy that rips away a smile off of my face like a leopard rips the rotting flesh of its prey. It causes my teeth to clench in the middle of my frustration. Look, there comes bitterness and sorrow, the siblings of anger! Here comes their mother and father, grief and depression. This dreadful family is what I endlessly try to avoid at all cost. Nevertheless, they continually try to hinder me.

No! Not another day will I allow the mouth of anger to consume me. No longer will I allow the stomach of anger to digest me and destroy me with its poisonous acids. No longer will I allow anger to have control over me. I will defeat it with a smile. With laughter, I will crush anger. With a song, I will annihilate the dreadful family, and I will destroy their house of gloom. Anger will no longer take residency in my heart. Its citizenship is denied, and its family is evicted from my soul. Today my spirit rejoices, because anger has been replaced by another.

Joy.

The Storm

Written By: Vernell Diamond II

I am not afraid of the storm,

Although it is fierce and endangering, I will not fear.

I am not afraid of the storm,

Although the wind is strong and causes me to stumble, I will bravely stand unafraid.

I will not fear the storm,

Although the rain seems uncontrollable and is blinding to my sight, I will fear nothing.

The storm is large and tremendously dangerous, but my God will command it to cease for my benefit. The thunder may roar as a vigorous lion, and the lightning may strike like a piercing arrow to its target, but still, I will stand. I will stand against the storm and its indescribable fury.

Though pain may visit me, I will rebuke it. Though misery may knock at my door, I will deny it. The venomous poison of depression has dried up like a weary tree in the peak of winter. The storm, I have endured, but at last, I see a silver lining. Morning has finally come.

Strange Woman

Written by: Vernell Diamond II

Who is that strange woman, so lovely, sweet and fair?

Her beauty is so mesmerizing that I'm severely tempted to stare.

Her hair is sheen and long, her eyes are filled with passion, and her body is so voluptuous filling my sight with satisfaction.

She is very attractive, but her intent is deceiving. Her demeanor is lustful, but extremely pleasing.

She makes me tremble and quake with desire, with a burning passion, a never-ending fire.

Who is this strange woman that I see on this screen? She's so far away, but close enough to affect my entire being.

My heart is pounding. My eyes are still, and my mind is focused on her against my will.

The fierceness of her presence and the softness of her voice has captivated me, and turning from her is my last choice.

Since my eyes have seen her, the memory can't be erased.

Although I want to, I'll never forget her gorgeous face.

She has attempted to rob me of my innocence, with her charming ways and her tempting presence.

Her lips have trapped me. Her eyes are my weakness. How can I escape from the soft hands of this temptress?

O Lord, save me from this strange woman now!

I'm too weak to resist, help me to deny her somehow!

I hate and despise her, and she has ruined me. She has blinded my focus away from my destiny.

Erase her from my memory; I want to forget her ways of debauchery. I want a good woman to view, righteous and holy.

Let this be my ultimate wish and my strongest demand; I don't want to see that strange woman today or ever again.

Where is it in the Bible? Proverbs 7

Sorrow of Man

Written by: Vernell Diamond II

This explains the sorrow of a man,

Who has walked away from God's plan.

His feet are trapped inside hardened clay,

For the Lord is whom he refuses to obey.

Now he is a wretch undone,

For he has denied God's only son.

His ordered steps are now memories,

For his path is covered with sinful misery.

This explains the sorrow of a man,

Who has totally ignored God's command.

Although he feels like he's drowning in sinking sand, God supplies him with another chance.

Though this man is stubborn to God's call,

God knows his problems which he is willing to solve.

This sorrowful man has a choice, whether to adhere to or ignore God's voice.

The savior will call as he may, but the man has to choose to walk in his way. This man's sorrow can turn to happiness, only if his iniquity transforms into holiness.

Restore Your Confidence

Written by: Vernell Diamond II

If your circumstances are making you weary,

Don't be discouraged,

Current times may make you dreary,

Please be encouraged.

Trouble doesn't last always,

Weeping endures only for the night,

Jesus will surely make a way,

Your soul will rejoice in his delight.

Satan thrives to destroy your confidence,

The confidence within you to grow,

God has given you great substance,

Satan can't stop its flow.

No weapon formed shall prosper,

Against any of God's sheep,

We'll walk in his pasture,

Our souls he will keep.

Restore your confidence,

Encourage yourself,

Lift up your countenance,

Grab that Bible on the shelf.

Read God's word and commands,

Let it feed your soul,

Obey his demands,

Then the blessings will unfold.

Keep your head up,

Let your heart and God's word mend,

And when the Satan persuades you to give up,

Remind him of his end.

Music

Written by: Vernell Diamond II

Music is something I can't live without.

It's something that I adore.

The sound of music excites me.

My ears hunger for more.

It makes my heart beat faster.

My eyes open wide.

My feet won't cease from tapping, and my emotions flow from inside.

Music is a part of my life.

It's built into my design.

The sound waves give me chills, vigorously trickling down my spine.

I appreciate music.

It's a passion I long for.

The rhythms move me,

The melodies I can't ignore.

My ears have witnessed many songs.

Many lyrics have exited my mouth,

Whether local or foreign,

From the north or from the south.

In my journey, I've discovered,

Music can be good or evil,

It depends on the intent that infiltrates the minds of people.

Some music is uplifting,

Some music is pleasing,

Some music angers the soul,

Also, some can be deceiving.

Some music is sensual,

It opens the door for lust,

Some music gives praise,

It is righteous, bold, and just.

The rhythm appeals to the ear,

But the lyrics give the message,

Pay attention to what is said,

You might learn a lesson.

Never listen to only the beat,

Yes, the melody is sweet,

The bass is concrete,

But without words, the song is incomplete.

Some people misuse music,

To control the emotions from within,

Some spread their music from coast to coast,

Simply to promote sin.

Some composers can mix several sounds,

They cause perfect harmonies to blend,

But how can people plead to know music without knowledge of its origin?

Music was invented by God,

It's meant for his praise,

Through music, I honor God only, day by day.

Music is God's gift to man,

It resonates powerfully at its finest,

Music that doesn't fulfill its duty is totally useless.

Music lifts and offers the mind and soul,

Unto what, is up to you,

My warning is this, be careful of what you listen to.

Protect Your Heart

Written by: Vernell Diamond II

Your heart is a glorious vessel,

It beats from deep inside,

It is an important house where love abides.

God uses the heart of men,

To reach the masses,

To teach them to love their neighbors,

And to forgive their enemy's trespasses.

Therefore, your heart is a target,

For the devil to attack and take,

He wants to replace love with hate.

Satan wants your whole heart to cause your destruction,

But God wants your whole heart for your glorious salvation.

Protect your heart from evil,

Stay away from sinful deeds,

God will guide you to righteousness,

He will also supply your needs.

God wants love to remain in your heart,

For his glory and your benefit,

For hate only destroys and is highly irrelevant.

Loneliness Will Not Define Me

Written by: Vernell Diamond II

Loneliness will not define me. Understand that loneliness is not just a feeling, but also a lifestyle. It is a disease that infiltrates the mind and devours self-esteem. Afterwards, it becomes the face of all of your reasoning and decisions. The pain of feeling like you have no one to count on will hover over you like a dreary storm cloud if you allow it. That is the pain that loneliness brings.

Loneliness will not define me. I won't let. It could easily destroy its prey, for loneliness is the predator. It is as a lion waiting to pounce upon its helpless victim. The feeling of having no one to put your trust in is miserable. The feeling that no one cares for you is dreadful. However, loneliness will not define me for I am never lonely. Even when I feel like no one knows of the trouble that I endure, I remember that I am never alone.

Jesus is with me. He is always beside me. Therefore, I can't be lonely. So when that lion called loneliness pounces to devour me, Jesus slays it for my benefit. He is the comforter when I need to be comforted. When loneliness tries to saturate my mind with grief, Jesus fills me with joy reminding me that he has watched over me since the beginning. Therefore loneliness in my life does not exist.

So, when you have no one to put your trust in, put your trust in Jesus. If you feel that no cares for you, remember that Jesus does, for his love is a river with no end. He showed that through his death for you. When humans fail you and leave you suddenly, don't fret. Your faith belongs in the hand of the Creator, not the creation. Jesus is the reason why loneliness will not define me. Don't let it define you.

Keep Moving On

Written by: Vernell Diamond II

Keep moving on people, never give up.

Keep moving on and keep your head up.

Keep moving on, don't forget your dreams.

Keep moving towards light no matter how dark it seems.

Keep moving teachers; the children need their education.

Keep moving preachers; people are saved through salvation.

Keep moving doctors, so that the sick can get well.

Keep moving judges, so that justice may prevail.

Keep moving fathers; provide for your families.

Keep moving mothers; raise your children with tranquility.

Keep moving pastors and lead your churches.

Keep moving saints; God needs your service.

Whatever you do, no matter how long,

Never give up, keep moving on.

I Am Human First

Written by: Vernell Diamond II

Why do you only see me as a black man? Why do you see me as different? I have a head like you. I have arms, legs, feet, eyes, ears, and a mouth just like you. We also have hearts that beat continually. So how am I different?

Don't think less of me because my skin is a darker shade than yours. I am human and so are you. I am not just a black man, I am human and do not deserve to be treated like I am nothing. God created humans equally. If God had that much sense, who would have the audacity or the right to say that their color changes equality? That is utter stupidity.

All nationalities are of the same species called humanity, which makes us all equal under one God. So don't label me by color, but by my nature of being human. Don't scrutinize me by stereotypes, but study me by my character and lifestyle. Yes, I am a colored American, but I am human first.

How Can I Go On?

Written by: Vernell Diamond II

How can I go on?

I'm at the brink of defeat,

My faith is shattered like glass underneath my feet.

How can I go on?

I am tired and weary,

Progress has stood still, and the days are quite dreary.

How can I go on?

My hands are clenched,

With fury, I grind my teeth in lament.

How can I stand?

How can I follow God's command, with an empty heart, with unclean hands?

Sorrow is an understatement.

I have worn it for a long time.

It hangs on me like chains on a prisoner guilty of crime.

Dread fills the ears of my mind.

It barks like a hound.

It croaks the most undesirable sounds.

Where is my relief?

My comfort has escaped.

My happiness has turned into utter disgrace.

Laughter is now groaning.

Smiles are currently frowns.

My life has gone from up to down.

How can I go on?

Only God knows.

My eyes can't see that far down the road.

God says I can overcome.

His word assures my victory,

But my mind thinks otherwise; my confidence is temporary.

I shouldn't speak this way,

But my feelings I can no longer hide.

I will not continue to wear a disguise.

My mask is burned.

Its ashes are erased.

But still my happiness is misplaced.

God of my fathers,

Heal my wounds,

My heart is broken and out of tune.

I must go on.

I must be made whole.

For much is at stake, including my soul.

So I'll continue to fight,

I'll stand strong,

I'll return to holiness where I belong.

Jesus is with me,

I'll stand on his promise,

And I will live the rest of my life as his witness.

Guard Your Soul

Written by: Vernell Diamond II

Be careful little boy of what you hear, your ears are precious and very sincere.

Be careful little girl of the words you speak, for they should not be harmful, but tender and meek.

Be careful young man of where you go; don't travel to places where evil flows.

Be careful young woman of what you wear, dress modestly or the wolves will stare.

Be careful Father of what you do, remember your children are watching you.

Be careful Mother of how you act; your children will follow your lead, and that's a fact.

Be mindful sinners of the time passing by, for soon Jesus will crack the sky.

Be careful saints of losing your fire; don't let Satan steal your righteous desires.

Be careful people of outer darkness; come to the light and precious holiness.

Be careful people; guard your souls that your destiny in Christ will gracefully unfold.

False Pretenses

Written by: Vernell Diamond II

Why do some show false pretenses?

Why do people wear masks?

Why do people hide the truth knowing the posing won't last?

Their true identity is exclusive.

No one knows their real personality.

Their genuine traits are hidden behind clouds of obscurity.

This shouldn't be.

Jesus is the true vine.

His life was not hidden behind disguise.

He was the same in public as he was at home.

He is still the same as he sits on the throne.

Follow his example.

Don't be a fake.

Be truthful and honest to all for your sake.

If your true identity is tarnished, let Jesus fix it.

Don't hide yourself because of humanistic judgment.

It is better to fix a problem than to mask it.

Consequences of an unresolved problem will be drastic.

Come to the realization that truth is just.

If you are not honest about who you are, no one will give you their trust.

Now if you're covered in false pretenses,

And you continually wear masks,

Throw that lifestyle away, that is your task.

A person of honor is a person of truth.

Give your life to Christ so that your true identity will be renewed.

Bed of Unrest

Written by: Vernell Diamond II

"A bed is for rest."

That's usually what they say.

However, for myself,

It doesn't turn out that way.

The nights seem long,

But the hours swiftly pass,

And my peaceful sweet dreams usually don't last.

My bed is a throne of thoughts, and a place for decisions,

Sometimes I am sent various dreams and visions.

I toss and I turn, and then I am still,

Often I'm awakened against my will.

My thoughts are racing,

My mind is a field, where battles between good and evil are held.

Sleep? What's that?

A pigment of my imagination,

I'm more awake in my dreams.

What a situation.

One o'clock, two o'clock, three o'clock, four,

Morning knocks at my door as my eyes grow sore.

A bed is for rest? I'll keep that in mind.

I hope that becomes true for me in due time.

A Woman Scorned

Written by: Vernell Diamond II

Who can comfort a woman scorned?

Who can hide her disgrace?

Who will wipe the thousands of tears that have fallen down her face?

Who can endure what she has?

Who can understand her pain?

How can she know joy again if only anger remains?

Who did this to her?

Who destroyed her self-esteem?

Who caused this damsel to feel unworthy, miserable and unclean?

Who made her eyes as red as blood?

Who filled them with frustration?

Who made her a helpless victim of spontaneous temptation?

Her eyes tell a thousand stories.

Her teeth clench in wrath.

Her anger burns like magma destroying everything in its path.

Her feet stomp in fury.

Ugly scars divide her heart.

She has made so many mistakes, and she longs for a new start.

Jesus, heal every scorned woman.

Forgive their sins.

Cleanse their hearts and everything else within.

Turn their frown into a smile.

Bring peace to their souls.

Make their broken hearts completely whole.

A woman scorned is a woman strong, and her story is like a well-written song.

Through her tribulation, she's a woman scorned, but in her testimony, she's a woman reborn.

Reflections of a Virgin

Written by: Vernell Diamond II

My purity is everything. I understand that in this modern era, it is extremely odd to cherish your purity enough to keep it, but my purity is everything. I understand that it is strange to many, but not to me. Ask me any question. Yes, I'm single. No, my lips have not tasted that of the opposite sex. No, I haven't experienced the pleasures of intimacy. No, my hands have not caressed the body of my love. My time will come, but until then my virginity will be kept, reserved for the marriage bed.

My virginity is my purity. It is as a flawless diamond shining in the midst of rhinestones. One day God will bless me with the woman he has destined for me to be with, but until then, I will remain pure.

My virginity is one of the most precious things in my possession. So why wouldn't I wait to surrender my precious gift to someone just as precious in a sacred marriage? Why would I throw my purity away as trash? Would an Olympian sell his gold medal? Would a king give his throne to a beggar? So why would I give my precious jewel to a harlot?

Until that blessed day, when I will be given into marriage to my love, my purity will rest upon me as a royal robe resting upon the shoulders of a mighty king. I will not cast my pearls to swine.

So go ahead and laugh at my status of being a virgin. I smile because my purity is with me, and I will gladly lay it down for a bride. Yes, I am single, yes, I am a virgin, and yes, my purity is everything.

Four

Tributes

Poems dedicated to extraordinary people in my life

Man of Many Wonders

To my loving and gracious Father

Written by: Vernell Diamond II

You're a man of wisdom, because in wisdom, you taught me to be a man. While experiencing the nature of life and the trials that life brings, you taught me how to get through them. With humility, you taught me to be humble. In righteousness, you taught me to be righteous. In wisdom, you helped to make me wise.

You're a man of peace, for in peace, you raised me. You showed me how to stand up for myself, and when to hold my tongue. You taught me how to treat others as I would want to be treated. You humbly helped others even when you needed help. That enabled me to follow in your footsteps.

You are a man of dominion. You have shown me how important it is to own and not to borrow. You showed me how to successfully maintain finances and a household to take care of a family. Now I have the ability to ensure security to my future family because of your example.

Most of all, you are a man of holiness. Every day, you walk faithfully in the ways of Christ. You've taught me his word and how to live by his statutes, and for that I am grateful.

You are a man of many wonders, and I know that God will reward you greatly for your diligence at the time to come. Thank you for being the greatest father a son could ever have.

I love you with all of my heart, and I am honored to be called your son.

Thank You

To My Loving Mother

Written by: Vernell Diamond II

I am grateful that God gave me the privilege to have such an excellent mother. Today I thank you for your many sacrifices you have displayed for my happiness. I thank you for your strength, carrying me in your womb until childbirth. I thank you for nurturing me as a child. I thank you for wiping every tear from my eyes, comforting me in my sorrow.

I thank you for every encouraging word of wisdom you have sown into my life. I thank you for being an excellent example. You have taught me the ways of Christ and have never taken a break from living holy.

The essence of your presence breathes life into anyone whom you encounter, because you approach all with love, and your countenance is righteous.

I pray that someday I can marry a wife who is as righteous, as kind, as loving, and as virtuous as you are. Lastly, if I don't say this enough to you, remember that I love you and will always be your son.

The Shepherd

To My Loving Pastor

Written by: Vernell Diamond II

You are a holy woman of God and a strong woman of faith. The power of God surrounds you like a mighty shield, and the Holy Ghost has saturated your entire being like a heavy rain watering the Earth.

Your words are wise, and your actions are just. Your deeds show the essence of a shepherd. You are someone who has tended sheep that have need of guidance. You are someone who has a heart to understand the worries of the forgotten and the down-trodden. You are someone who has made straight the way of the Lord while leading his precious little ones into their destiny.

Don't worry, you will not go unrewarded. You are a shepherd among shepherds, and when the Chief Shepherd shall appear, you will receive a crown of glory that will not fade away.

Fight on, O faithful shepherd, you will not go unrewarded. You are my Pastor, and I wouldn't change that for anything.

With love, your son in Christ.

Forever, Our Beloved

Written by: Vernell Diamond II

In honor of my cousin, Minister Marvin Coffey

He was a thought conceived by the mind of God since the foundation of Earth,

He was a baby formed in his mother's womb that came into the world at birth.

He was a gifted child with a brilliant mind and he played with blessed hands,

He could fix, build, and create many things, even as a man.

As a man, he was baptized and filled with the spirit of our Lord Jesus Christ,

He would then follow our savior, Jesus, for the rest of his life.

He was a man of family, laughter, love, and he wore a smile so divine,

He sang with a voice more wonderful than the stars among the skies.

He was a man of God that preached the good news any chance that he could,

He served his master faithfully like any servant should.

He is gone now, but he lives again, embraced in love,

He has traveled to yonder place, to that great city above.

Throughout his life, he prayed to his Lord, who sits on the throne,

And now he has seen that same Lord who has welcomed him home.

Although we will miss our good friend, we'll send him our love,

For he was, is, and forever will be, our beloved.

Two Gloves

In loving memory of my cousins, Marvin and Richard Coffey

Written by: Vernell Diamond II

I hate to see loved ones go. Their passing usually leaves an empty feeling in my heart. I guess it's because they're missing now. The deaths of these two particular individuals were odd though because they were close to me. Furthermore, I helped bury them about a year apart, and both weren't older than fifty. It hurts to see them go so young. Their lives were as vapor that floats into the air and vanishes. If there was some way that I could preserve that vapor, I would. Nonetheless, when God says time's up, it's time to go on to the next life.

I am going to miss my cousins and their warming smiles. I will miss the laughs we had. I will miss the conversations we shared. Their smiles and words of wisdom will never be forgotten. The truth is that I love them very much. I had the honor to bury them both. On each casket, I placed a glove from my left hand. The glove I placed, in my eyes, represents the hand that carried them to their place of rest. The glove on my right hand represents the love they have shown me that touches me every day. So in gratitude I gladly gave them honor. I watched as my glove, along with the casket, descending into the Earth. They came from the dust, and to the dust they returned. I hope that I will see them both again, and I pray that I will never have to lay down another glove again.

Five

Short Story Poems

Sarah's Purpose

Written by: Vernell Diamond II

There was a woman named Sarah, a humble lady was she,

She loved the Lord Jesus and served him diligently.

She was barren for a while, and she prayed for a child,

But her wait was so lengthy that it put her in denial.

"I'll never have a child," said Sarah. "How long do I have to wait?"

Her husband comforted her saying, "Sarah, where is your faith?"

"God's time is not ours," he said. "He knows what's best for us."

Then Sarah replied, "I'll wait longer if I must."

In a year's time, Sarah gave birth to a girl.

She was so precious, and she brightened Sarah's world.

"We'll name her Hannah," Sarah said, as her husband softly kissed her forehead.

Time has passed, now Hannah's ten, and Sarah's husband is preaching in the Cayman Islands.

Sarah and Hannah live together in New York City with cold weather.

Sarah's heart is filled with gladness. God brought her heart out of sadness.

He blessed her with the child whom she always wanted.

Since then, she has never taken faith for granted.

On a cold day when the weather was cruel, Sarah was taking Hannah to school.

The wind was high, and it started to grow as Hannah stared and her eyes began to glow.

With seat belts buckled and car ready, Sarah pulled off smoothly and steady.

"Mommy I see your job," Hannah stated, as Sarah passed her bakery where her customers waited.

As Sarah drove through the intersection, traffic became thick from every direction.

"Hold tight sweetie," Sarah replied, as the intersection grew far and wide.

Their car turned left on a side road, and behind them was a truck carrying a heavy load.

Ice was thick upon the ground that day, which is why traffic formed a heavy delay.

The driver in front was distracted as she pulled up to a stop sign and suddenly reacted.

She slammed on the breaks and came to a stop. Sarah repeated the action causing her head to flop.

Sarah and the driver in front stopped riding, but the truck behind wasn't able to and went sliding.

BAM! The truck hit Sarah's car, pushing her vehicle into the first one extremely hard.

Dented in the front and folded across the back, it looked like Sarah's car had been attacked.

Horns sounded and sirens too, as people ran toward the wreck two by two.

Sarah awaking wounded and dazed, started looking around her desperately amazed.

"Are you okay?" the people screamed. Sarah shook her head up and down as she viewed the scene.

While gasping for air, it came to mind, that she wasn't the only one in the car during this time.

As she looked behind while trying to stand, all that she could see, was Hannah's right hand.

The rest of her body was severely smashed by the back of the car that nearly folded in half.

Screaming lament came from Sarah as she desperately tried to save her daughter.

"Hannah," she continually cried, as she kissed the hand of her child who has died.

Sarah awakens in a hospital bed, looking at her hands that are bloody red.

"Where is my baby?" Sarah insisted. She looks to the nurse who has patients listed.

Sarah's name is on the list of patients to be released, but Hannah's name is on the list of the deceased.

"I'm sorry about your loss," the nurse said with gloom, and then she solemnly walked out of the room.

"Why God," Sarah cried. "Why did you let my baby die?"

"I waited so long for her to get here, and now I have to bury her after ten years."

One year has passed, Sarah and her husband are together, still mourning that their girl is gone forever.

Sarah's faith is gone and her head is down, praying to God to bring Hannah back somehow.

She went to sleep and had a dream one night, and what she saw gave her a fright.

She was standing in front of God's throne, with no one around, standing alone.

On the side of the throne stood a child who was very young and very mild.

Sarah humbly bowed before the Lord. "Where is my child?" she implored.

The child stepped up into the light. "Hannah," she screamed with all of her might!

As Sarah ran to Hannah, an angel appeared, gripping Sarah with great fear.

"What do you want?" Sarah said while kneeling and covering her head.

The angel stood tall and bright glowing with a brilliant light.

"I am Hannah's guardian angel on Earth and now here. I come in peace and there is no need to fear."

The angel said this peacefully as Hannah stood by quietly.

Sarah stood and shouted with dismay, "Why didn't you protect Hannah that day?"

The angel replied, "It was her time. God allowed your child to die."

Sarah replied, "Why did he? Why did he let this terrible thing be?"

"This moment isn't terrible," the angel replied. "Your daughter now lives in paradise."

Sarah replied, "But we miss her so. Her father and I couldn't even watch her grow.

She died so soon and left us to mourn. We prayed for her, even before she was born."

"There is a purpose to everything," the angel shared. "God won't put more on you than you can bear.

He took Hannah for a reason, and his reason is just. In him, you should put all of your trust.

Sarah, ask God about your purpose, so that your testimony will help others in surplus."

After this was said, Sarah raised her head and realized that she was back in bed.

She immediately fell on her knees, and asked, "What is my purpose? Tell me Lord, please.

What is the reason for Hannah leaving, and my husband and I are stuck here grieving?"

For seven nights, she prayed that prayer and the Lord looked upon her with care.

He was with her the whole time with their beautiful family in his mind.

One Monday morning, there was a knock at the door. It was a customer from Sarah's bakery store.

"What is it Rachel?" asked Sarah with concern. Rachel had a bandage on her arm that was severely burned.

"My house burned down a week ago, and everyone survived except my baby boy Joe."

Rachel said this with grief and her head hanging down while Sarah stared at her with a frown.

"I'm sorry for your loss," Sarah said. "Please don't cry and hold up your head.

It will get better, and God will comfort you. He will ease your pain and see you through."

Rachel replied carefully, "Will you state my son's eulogy?"

Sarah replied, "Yes I surely can." Sarah didn't know that this was part of God's plan.

At the funeral, it was Sarah's turn to speak. She began to start the eulogy she had been preparing for a week.

"Greetings to all and my condolences to the bereaved, I pray that God puts your pain at ease.

I am here to give encouragement to the family of Joe Johnson in precious humility.

I know that it hurts that your son is gone, and the feeling of it all may seem wrong.

Your question may be like mine. Why God, did you let my child die?

However, we shouldn't question God on his plan, because his wisdom is infinite compared to man.

So please don't grieve but celebrate Joe's life and be happy that he now lives in paradise.

Pray that God gives you peace, and that he will set your troubled minds at ease.

Don't forget that God lost his son too, and he had a time of grieving just like you.

With time, you will heal, and you will gain happiness, so remember the good times with gladness.

Joe Johnson is now safe my friends, and hopefully one day you will see him again."

The crowd cheered and applauded with joy, as it were a celebration for the baby boy.

Rachel said to Sarah, "Thank you so much, that message gave me strength and everyone was touched."

Sarah returned home and she hugged her spouse, and she sat down with him on the couch.

"I know what I want to do," Sarah said. "I know my purpose, I am spirit lead."

"I want to minister to those that are grieved; who have lost loved ones and are bereaved.

I'll start a foundation that builds funds for families that have lost loved ones"

"I'm proud of you," her husband said gladly. "Do what God leads you to do and do it carefully."

Afterwards, Sarah started a foundation, and she was excited for all the generous donations.

"Hannah's Hand" was its name, and in New York City, it had great fame.

The proceeds went to families that lost their beloved. The symbol was a hand releasing a dove.

Therapists were paid to see anyone that needed therapy if they lost loved ones.

Classes were set to teach families of how to regain faith and happiness after someone's passing.

Furthermore, many witnessed the love of Christ, and many received him and gained eternal life.

Sarah's bakery funds helped with the proceeds, and her husband's ministry funds also helped the foundation succeed.

"Hannah's Hand" was a success, and the community supported it with their best.

This was the reason that Hannah had to go, that Sarah's ministry could grow.

Sarah had a mission to help others to get through the problem that she suffered.

Now it is clear to what was in God's mind. Sarah's purpose had to come to life in due time.

The Man at Resurrection Bridge

Written by: Vernell Diamond II

In a large city stood an idle bridge, tall, wide, and unable to be hid.

Its reputation stood alone as an abyss of horrid evil unknown.

Wicked sin was normality in this city, and God himself looked upon it with pity.

This hedonistic waste land displayed temporary pleasure; the stench of its sin slowly began to fester.

The souls of people in the city became empty, because pleasure was not enough to fill their hearts with serenity.

Many citizens were struck with depression; so they went to the bridge to relieve their oppression.

SUICIDE gave the bridge its fame, and Suicide Bridge became its name.

Nevertheless, no one knew that one man would not let this continue.

His name was Gabe, a mysterious man; he came from nowhere, but he had a plan.

His long gray hair flickered in the wind, as did the fire of God in him flowing from within.

On the bridge, he stood with a Bible in his hand, and he only spoke when God gave the command.

He preached to every soul that was depressed with life, about his Lord and savior Jesus Christ.

He told everyone that was sinfully oppressed, that Jesus would save them and give them rest.

Gabe persuaded the masses to deny death, but to rely on the Holy Spirit for divine help.

Suicide decreased until it completely ceased, and that city was inhabited with glorious peace.

Death lost its sting and was defeated suddenly; Gabe completed his task in great victory.

Todd Avery, a new minister in town, heard the great news going around.

He yearned to join Gabe on his mission, so he went to the bridge to receive permission.

"The Lord be praised,' cried Gabe,' and let his glory reign always."

The faithful two went into a ministry together, persuading all to follow Jesus forever.

Gabe trained Todd to preach, and many souls Todd surely reached.

However, after six months of the ministry with Todd, Gabe received a word from God.

"My time here is done,' proclaimed Gabe,' it is God's will and I must obey."

"I've trained you well so you know what to do and always remember that God is with you."

Todd knew that their partnership would rend, so he solemnly said, "Farewell my friend."

Gabe walked slowly toward the end of the road as the tears in Todd's eyes began to flow.

Gabe turned around and calmly smiled, and then he glanced at the sky for a while.

Then he raised his hands to the rising sun and shouted loudly, "Occupy until the Lord comes!"

Gabe walked away until he was out of sight, but his departure gave Todd a fright,

For Todd saw a figure burst into the sky, speeding through the clouds many miles high.

From that moment on, Todd knew the importance of the task that he had to do.

It took an anointed and righteous man to lead this city back to God's plan.

Todd continued where Gabe had finished, and joy in the city was replenished.

Suicide Bridge became Resurrection Bridge, and the testimony of that city was never hid.

Made in the USA
Columbia, SC
20 April 2019